Prayers that Stir
the Hearts
of Grandparents

Sherry Schumann

Prayers that Stir the Hearts of Grandparents

Requests for information should be sent to:
Sherry Schumann
sherry@christiangrandparenting.net
s3bjschu@ymail.com
www.sherryschumann.com

ISBN: 9781690833192

DEDICATION

This book is dedicated to...

Our sons and daughters-in-law
Skip and Lauren, Brandon and Julie, Jairus and Sarah

Our adorable grandchildren
Anne Louise, Hank, Sally, Wyatt and Frances

Our other grandchildren, yet to be born

Praying for you is an honor and privilege.
One of life's greatest JOYS!

CONTENTS

ACKNOWLEDGMENTS

Deborah Haddix

Thank you for your keen insight, wise council and loving insistence that I assemble these prayers into a book. God chuckled the day we met, knowing that you would become my editor, publisher and more importantly, one of my best friends.

Lillian Penner and Cavin Harper, Cathy Jacobs and Peter Rothermel

Thank you for inviting me to join you on this incredible journey. Already, it's been the adventure of a lifetime. The greatest part of working with Christian Grandparenting Network and the Diocese of SC is serving alongside my spiritual giants, namely the four of you.

Larry Fowler and my friends at Legacy Coalition

Thank you for inviting me to post prayers for grandparents on your Facebook page. Your invitation is the impetus behind this project.

John Coulombe

Thank you for helping me recognize that being a prayer warrior is a calling given to each of us.

My beloved husband, Sammy

Next to our Lord and Savior, there's no one I love like you.

A LEGACY OF PRAYER

You can spot them from a distance. They amble through the superstore, their shopping carts overflowing with precariously stacked baby products and toddler toys. "Ask me," they scream silently. "Ask me if I'm a new grandparent."

I oblige them by asking. I admire picture-after-picture as these precious new grandparents scroll through the albums on their phone. I inwardly chuckle, wondering if their iCloud is saturated. I listen attentively as they show me the items they're purchasing, just to tide the baby over until they get a chance to "really shop."

I am attentive, because I am genuinely interested. I was that grandparent six years ago when our oldest granddaughter was born. I remember needing to tell someone, anyone, even a perfect stranger standing at the checkout line, that I was a new grandmother. My heart couldn't contain the love, which I was feeling.

If I offer these precious new grandparents any advice, it's the following: While there's nothing wrong with purchasing name-brand strollers or cribs, American Girl dolls or top-grade soccer balls, the greatest gift that we can give our children can't be purchased online or picked up at a big-box store. It won't break, corrode, deteriorate, fray or rot. It costs nothing, except time and commitment on our part. The greatest gift is the gift of prayer.

Two years ago, Legacy Coalition asked if I would submit a weekly prayer for their Facebook page. This book is a collection of forty of my favorite prayers.

I invite you to look first at the Table of Contents. You will notice that the prayers are listed in alphabetical order, by topic. Most of the prayers pertain to our grandchildren; however, there are some prayers for our adult children, namely their parents, and for us.

I also invite you to flip through the pages of the book. You'll notice that the left-hand page contains the prayers, and the right-hand page is nothing more than lined space. This layout is very intentional on my part. I want to encourage you to do more than read the prayers; I want you to engage with them. I want these prayers to become your prayers.

I recommend you familiarize yourself with each prayer by reading it aloud. Be aware of what I call "inaudible whispers" or a quickening of the heart as the Holy Spirit speaks to you. Use the blank lines on the right-hand page to personalize the prayer in one of the following ways:

1) List any thoughts, concerns, Scripture verses or thanksgivings, which came to mind, as you read the prayer aloud.
2) Rewrite the prayer, inserting your grandchildren's names into the words "our grandchildren."
3) Rewrite the entire prayer, using your words instead of mine, the Scriptures you have chosen and the names of your grandchildren. Don't forget to include the things the Holy Spirit revealed to you.

These prayers are yours to pray with boldness and certainty that our God listens and attends to the voice of our prayers. He doesn't reject our prayers, and He doesn't hold His steadfast love from us (Psalm 66:19-20, paraphrased).

One final note: These prayers were written with more than one grandparent in mind. If you are praying alone, please change the plural pronouns "we" and "us" to their singular form, that is "I" and "me."

PRAYERS

Apple of God's Eye

Every good and every perfect gift is from above (James 1:17).

Heavenly Father,

We glorify You for all the blessings of this life, especially our precious grandchildren. They are the apple of our eye, and they bring us indescribable joy.

More importantly, they are the "apple of Your eye" (Deuteronomy 32:10). You knew them before they were formed in the womb. (Jeremiah 1:5). You engraved them on the palms of Your hands (Isaiah 49:16), and You rejoice over them with loud singing (Zephaniah 3:17).

Thank you, LORD, for "every good and perfect gift is from above" (James 1:17), and that includes our grandchildren.

We pray in Jesus' Name.

Amen.

_____

_____

_____

_____

_____

_____

_____

_____

_____

_____

_____

_____

_____

_____

_____

_____

_____

_____

_____

_____

_____

_____

_____

_____

_____

_____

_____

Armor of God

Put on the whole armor of God, that you may be able to stand against the schemes of the devil (Ephesians 6:11).

Lord Jesus,

We find ourselves in a battle. The battle isn't "against flesh and blood, but against the rulers, against the authorities, against the cosmic powers over this present darkness" (Ephesians 6:12). Forgive us for the countless times we've attempted to handle this battle alone.

Cover us in the mantle of Your love. Cloak us in Your armor, securing it in place with the belt of Your truth. Safeguard our hearts against the world's depravity with the breastplate of Your righteousness. Shod our feet to stand firmly for Your gospel of peace. Protect our minds from Satan's lies with the helmet of Your salvation.

In all circumstances, show us how to use Your shield of faith to extinguish Satan's fiery darts. Show us how to disarm all forces of evil with Your sword of the Spirit, which is the Word of God (Ephesians 6:11-17).

Urge us to be persistent in prayer, "praying at all times in the Spirit, with all prayer and supplication" (Ephesians 6:18).

And remind us, with every breath we take, that You have already won the victory!

In your Name, we pray.

Amen.

Bullying

The LORD is near to the brokenhearted and saves the crushed in spirit (Psalm 34:18).

Lord Jesus,

You abhor bullying. You detest "haughty eyes, a lying tongue, hands that shed innocent blood, a heart that devises wicked schemes, feet that are quick to rush into evil, a false witness who pours out lies and a person who stirs up conflict in the community" (Proverbs 6:16-19, *NIV*).

Today we pray that You protect our grandchildren against gossip, harmful teasing and bullying. Place your armor upon them—Your belt of truth, Your breastplate of righteousness, Your shoes of readiness to stand for the Gospel of peace, Your shield of faith, Your helmet of salvation and Your sword of the Holy Spirit, which is the Word of God (Ephesians 6:13-18). Shield their hearts and minds from hurtful words, insults, lies and pranks.

We also pray for the classroom bullies. We can't begin to imagine what inner turmoil drives them to enjoy intimidating and humiliating others. Please forgive them, Lord, and heal them from the pain they too must be suffering.

In Your Name,

Amen.

Christmas (1)

And the Word became flesh and dwelt among us, and we have seen his glory, glory as of the only Son[a] from the Father, full of grace and truth (John 1:14).

Heavenly Father,

We confess that, both as a nation and as individuals, we have lost sight of Christmas' true meaning. We confess that we've prepared our homes instead of our hearts. We confess that we've preoccupied ourselves with To Do lists instead of contemplating Christ's Incarnation. We confess that we've decorated our mantles with lush greenery instead of remembering the dried straw on which Jesus lay. We confess that we've perused cookie recipes instead of immersing ourselves in the Word of God. We confess that we've chased an emotion instead of seeking the Truth. We confess that we've shared greeting cards and gifts without sharing the Good News; we've wished our neighbors "Happy Holidays" without wishing them "Merry Christmas!"

Please forgive us and guide us as we endeavor to put Christ back into Christmas!

In Christ's Name, we pray.

Amen.

Christmas (2)

For to us a child is born, to us a son is given; and the government shall be upon his shoulder, and his name shall be called Wonderful Counselor, Mighty God, Everlasting Father, Prince of Peace (Isaiah 9:6).

Heavenly Father,

We live in a culture, which encourages our grandchildren to be self-absorbed and self-centered, seeking instant gratification for their whims and desires. We see this during the holiday season, especially.

Please turn our grandchildren's hearts and minds from the world view of Christmas, namely marketing and commercialism, to the wonder and joy of that first Christmas morn. Let them, like the shepherds, gaze into Jesus' manger and behold the greatest Gift of all.

In Christ's Name, we pray.

Amen.

_____

_____

_____

_____

_____

_____

_____

_____

_____

_____

_____

_____

_____

_____

_____

_____

_____

_____

_____

_____

_____

_____

_____

_____

_____

_____

_____

Conquerors

For I am sure that neither death nor life, nor angels nor rulers, nor things present nor things to come, nor powers, nor height nor depth, nor anything else in all creation, will be able to separate us from the love of God in Christ Jesus our Lord (Romans 8:38-39).

Abba Father,

Please let our grandchildren understand that nothing can separate them from Your mercy or love, which is found in Christ Jesus… not family break-ups, academic struggles, peer pressure, persecution, angels or demons, or past mistakes. Not even death, itself. (Romans 8:37-39)

Let them know that "in all these things (they) are more than conquerors" through Jesus Christ, our Lord.

In Christ's Name, we pray.

Amen.

_____

_____

_____

_____

_____

_____

_____

_____

_____

_____

_____

_____

_____

_____

_____

_____

_____

_____

_____

_____

_____

_____

_____

_____

_____

_____

_____

_____

_____

Contentment

"But godliness with contentment is great gain" (I Timothy 6:6).

Abba Father,

We live in a culture where we are being pushed to jump higher, reach further and secure more things. Things that will never satisfy or fulfill us. Things that will enslave us to keep jumping higher, reaching further and securing more things. Things like adoration and acclamation, possessions and social status.

Today, we pray for ourselves, our children and our grandchildren. Help us to stop storing treasures on earth, where moth and rust destroy and where thieves break in and steal. Help us to store treasures in heaven, where neither moth nor rust destroys and where thieves do not break in and steal. For where our treasure is, there our hearts will be also (Matthew 6:19-21, paraphrased).

Keep our hearts in You!

In Jesus' Name, we pray.

Amen.

_____
_____
_____
_____
_____
_____
_____
_____
_____
_____
_____
_____
_____
_____
_____
_____
_____
_____
_____
_____
_____
_____
_____
_____
_____
_____
_____

Decisions

I will instruct you and teach you in the way you should go; I will counsel you with my eye upon you. (Psalm 32:8)

Dearest Lord Jesus,

You know every decision our grandchildren will face, the simple ones, the complicated ones and the ones with the potential to harm.

Let them get in the habit of turning to You every time they face difficult decisions. And give them the ability to distinguish Your voice saying, "This is the way; walk in it" (Isaiah 30:21).

In Your Name,

Amen.

_____

_____

_____

_____

_____

_____

_____

_____

_____

_____

_____

_____

_____

_____

_____

_____

_____

_____

_____

_____

_____

_____

_____

_____

_____

_____

_____

Easter

"Behold, the Lamb of God. He was pierced for our transgressions and crushed for our iniquities; by his wounds, we are healed (Isaiah 53:5).

Heavenly Father,

We pray our grandchildren comprehend the true meaning of Easter, even at a young age. Let them understand that this church holiday has nothing to do with egg hunts, spring fashions or chocolate-covered Cadbury bunnies. Let them understand that Jesus, in perfect obedience, offered himself as a sacrifice for our sins. Let them grasp the significance of the empty tomb, that He conquered death and reigns at Your right hand. Let them worship Him as King of Kings and Lord of Lords.

We pray our grandchildren celebrate Easter—the divine work of Jesus Christ's cross, resurrection and ascension—today and forevermore.

In Christ's Name, we pray.

Amen.

Enemy

And lead us not into temptation; but, deliver us from evil (Matthew 6:3).

Heavenly Father,

The enemy is a counterfeit fisherman, angling for his prey. He cast his lies and jiggles his bait, hoping to reel-in another unsuspecting soul.

Please rescue our children and grandchildren. Rescue them from being enamored and entangled in witchcraft, divination, magic, the world of enchantments and the occult. Rescue them from becoming hooked on alcohol, cigarettes, drugs, gambling or pornography. Rescue them from being schooled in the lie that Jesus is nothing more than social reform. Rescue them from snatching the bait that "If everyone else is doing it, it must be okay." Rescue them from drifting aimlessly without a purpose.

Rescue our children and grandchildren from the enemy's snares, and when necessary, rescue them from themselves.

In Christ's name, we pray.

Amen!

Faith

So, faith comes from hearing, and hearing through the word of Christ (Romans 10:17)

Lord Jesus,

We pray for the strengthening of our grandchildren's faith. Let them believe that You are the Christ, the Savior of the world. Let them grow in faith each time they hear or read God's Word. Let them be of courage, as they dare to be different from their peers, walking "by faith and not by sight" (2 Corinthians 5:7). Let them exercise their faith, using their gifts to spread the Gospel message throughout the world.

Let them join us in "the race that is set before us, looking to You, the founder and perfecter of our faith" (Hebrews 12:1-:2).

In Your Name, we pray.

Amen.

_____

_____

_____

_____

_____

_____

_____

_____

_____

_____

_____

_____

_____

_____

_____

_____

_____

_____

_____

_____

_____

_____

_____

_____

_____

_____

_____

False Doctrine

Do not be conformed to this world, but be transformed by the renewal of your mind, that by testing you may discern what is the will of God, what is good and acceptable and perfect (Romans 12:2).

Abba Father,

Today, we stand in the gap, praying for our grandchildren and their parents. Protect them from false teachings and doctrines, which are creeping stealthily into our schools and churches, workplaces and government offices. Protect them from relativism, the belief that there is no such thing as absolute truth.

Let our grandchildren and their parents understand the consequence of sin and their subsequent need for Jesus as their Savior. Let them confess and repent of their sins with the assurance that You are "faithful and just to forgive (their) sins and to cleanse (them) from all unrighteousness" (I John 1:9). Let them believe unequivocally that Jesus is "the Way and the Truth and the Life" (John 14:6).

In Christ Name, we pray.

Amen.

_____

_____

_____

_____

_____

_____

_____

_____

_____

_____

_____

_____

_____

_____

_____

_____

_____

_____

_____

_____

_____

_____

_____

_____

Father's Day

Fathers, do not provoke your children to anger, but bring them up in the discipline and instruction of the Lord (Ephesians 6:4).

Abba Father,

Today, we pray and give thanks for our grandchildren's earthly fathers. We pray that, like David, they will be men after Your own heart, men walking in obedience to Your will. Let them draw deeper into Christ's love every day.

We pray they rely on You for the wisdom, courage, knowledge and skills they need to be good parents and strong role models. Guide them as they provide for their family's physical, emotional and spiritual needs. Help them protect their loved ones by drawing safe and healthy boundaries.

We pray they actively and lovingly engage in their children's lives. Let them teach and guide through their own example of godly living, not provoking their children to anger but "bringing them up in the discipline and instruction of the Lord" (Ephesians 6:4). Let their words and actions consistently point to Your love, forgiveness, mercy and grace.

Bless them with hearts that are overflowing with love for You and their families.

In Christ's Name, we pray.

Amen.

_____

_____

_____

_____

_____

_____

_____

_____

_____

_____

_____

_____

_____

_____

_____

_____

_____

_____

_____

_____

_____

_____

_____

_____

_____

Friendships

A sweet friendship refreshes the soul" (Proverbs 27:9, The Message)

Dearest Lord Jesus,

We pray that you bless our grandchildren with sweet, long-lasting friendships. Bless them with friends who have positive attitudes, unquestionable integrity and sound judgment. Bless our grandchildren with sensitive, loving and wise hearts, so that they too can be friends with positive attitudes, unquestionable integrity and sound judgement.

And let them realize that the most precious, loving, long-lasting friendship they'll ever enjoy is with you.

In Your Precious Name, we pray.

Amen.

_____

_____

_____

_____

_____

_____

_____

_____

_____

_____

_____

_____

_____

_____

_____

_____

_____

_____

_____

_____

_____

_____

_____

_____

_____

_____

_____

_____

Future Grandchildren

For you formed my inward parts; you knitted me together in my mother's womb (Psalm 139:13).

Heavenly Father,

Today, we pray for our grandchildren and great-grandchildren, our future generations, yet to be born.

Your Word tells us that You know them before their first breath, their embryonic development or even their conception, Their names are inscribed in the palms of Your Son's nail-scarred hands (Jeremiah 1:5). Their days, every one of them, are recorded in Your book of life (Psalm 139:16). Such knowledge is almost too wonderful for us to comprehend.

We pray You protect our grandchildren and great-grandchildren from being unwanted, neglected or cast out of their mother's womb. Let their births be uncomplicated and uneventful, and let all who witness this splendid event praise You for the miracle of life.

In Jesus' Name, we pray.

Amen.

Grandparents Around the Globe

They who wait for the LORD shall renew their strength (Isaiah 40:31).

Dear God,

Thank you for the grandparents who selflessly offer their time, resources and hearts to their grandchildren.

Help them be the best grandparents they can be. Give them wisdom and discernment, as they strive to find a balance between being too strict or lenient. Help them navigate time constraints, financial worries and difficult family dynamics, in order to build long-lasting relationships with their grandchildren. Show them how to love their children and grandchildren as You love them, unconditionally and without reservation or restraint.

Let these dedicated grandparents give You thanks for the indescribable joy their grandchildren bring to this season of their lives. And please let them hear You say, "Well done, good and faithful servant" (Matthew 25:21).

In Jesus' Name, we pray.

Amen.

Grief

He will swallow up death forever; and the Lord God will wipe away tears from all faces (Isaiah 25:8).

Heavenly Father,

We approach You on bended knees, our hearts heavy for those who grieve from loss. Whether it's one less chair at the dining room table or a phone that doesn't ring, the reminder of a loved one who has passed is painful, sometimes even cruel.

We pray You comfort those who mourn. When their heartache becomes more than they can bear, please hide them in the cleft of Your rock.

We pray You give them courage to face one more moment, one more hour and one more day. Please give them "a crown of beauty instead of ashes, the oil of joy instead of mourning, and a garment of praise instead of a spirit of despair" (Isaiah 61:3).

In Christ's Holy Name we pray,

Amen.

_____

_____

_____

_____

_____

_____

_____

_____

_____

_____

_____

_____

_____

_____

_____

_____

_____

_____

_____

_____

_____

_____

_____

_____

_____

_____

_____

_____

Handiwork of God (1)

Does not the potter have the right to make out of the same lump of clay some pottery for special purposes and some for common use? (Romans 9:21, NIV)

Heavenly Father,

You are the potter; we are the clay. You knew and loved us before You made the world (Jeremiah 1:5). You fashioned and designed us according to your perfect plan.

We pray our grandchildren understand that they are your workmanship. Let them embrace this knowledge without rebellion, grumbling or complaint. Let them stop comparing themselves to their peers in the classroom, on the ballfield, in the dance class or on social media. Let them stop striving to attain the unattainable model of perfection, which is falsely pictured in advertisements, movies and television shows.

Instead, let them blossom in the knowledge that they are unique, designed for a specific purpose and loved by You, their Creator.

Thank You, God.

Amen.

Handiwork of God (2)

For we are his workmanship, created in Christ Jesus for good works, which God prepared beforehand, that we should walk in them (Ephesians 2:10).

Heavenly Father,

Our grandchildren are uniquely Yours. They are Your handiwork, wired according to Your perfect design. While one of our grandchildren spends hours converting an unsightly lump of clay into a masterpiece, another dismantles an object to discover how it works. While one shinnies up a tree in the blink of an eye, another insists that we read "just one more book." While one appears shy in large crowds, another has the innate ability to make us laugh.

We pray that You help us to know and understand our grandchildren as You do. Open our eyes to recognize and encourage them to cultivate their God-ordained personality traits, gifts and talents. Help us to serve as conduits of your unconditional love, speaking blessings into their lives and encouraging them to be all that You created them to be.

Thank you for making our grandchildren, just the way they are!

Amen.

Hearts of Flesh

And I will remove the heart of stone from your flesh and give you a heart of flesh (Ezekiel 36:27).

Abba Father,

Please redeem any brokenness, which prevents us from enjoying a close relationship with our children and grandchildren. Create opportunities for us to spend quality time with them—whether in person, by phone, through letters or via the Internet. Keep us from being judgmental and nagging. If there is any hardness in our hearts, please remove it. Give us hearts of flesh filled with acceptance and love.

Thank you, Father.

Amen.

_____

_____

_____

_____

_____

_____

_____

_____

_____

_____

_____

_____

_____

_____

_____

_____

_____

_____

_____

_____

_____

_____

_____

_____

_____

Heavy Burdens

Come to me, all who labor and are heavy laden, and I will give you rest (Matthew 11:28).

Lord Jesus,

Our hearts ache for our grandchildren, who are burdened and heavy laden. Some of them contend with the challenge of learning disabilities, while others grapple with the demands of scholarly perfection. Some are exhausted from hectic schedules, while others are aimless, getting into trouble because they have nothing to occupy their time. Some of them live in homes turned upside-down by broken marriages, while others are being raised by single parents. Some of them are emotionally abandoned, while others are smothered in their parents' love.

We pray our grandchildren come to you for rest. Let them relinquish the encumbrances they carry in exchange for the yoke you offer. "For (Your) yoke is easy, and (Your) burden light. (Matthew 11:30).

In your precious Name, we pray.

Amen.

_____
_____
_____
_____
_____
_____
_____
_____
_____
_____
_____
_____
_____
_____
_____
_____
_____
_____
_____
_____
_____
_____
_____
_____
_____
_____
_____
_____
_____
_____

Intentionality

"Not by might, nor by power, but by my Spirit," says the LORD of hosts *(Zechariah 4:6).*

Abba Father,

We fail in our feeble attempts to be intentional Christian grandparents. We give "urgent matters" priority over the important things in life. We fail to pray for our grandchildren's salvation, forget to share our faith stories when opportunities arise and stumble in our efforts to model Christ-like behavior. We forget to impress upon our grandchildren the depth of God's love.

Today, we recommit ourselves as intentional Christian grandparents, reminding ourselves that we "can do all things through Him, who strengthens (us)" (Philippians 4:13).

In Your Son's Name, we pray,

Amen.

_____

_____

_____

_____

_____

_____

_____

_____

_____

_____

_____

_____

_____

_____

_____

_____

_____

_____

_____

_____

_____

_____

_____

_____

_____

_____

_____

Lifelong Learners

"For the LORD gives wisdom; from his mouth come knowledge and understanding" *(Proverbs 2:6).*

Heavenly Father,

We pray our grandchildren strive to do their best at school. Let them be courteous, cooperative and respectful of their teachers and classmates as they take part in classroom activities and discussions. Let them approach their studies, especially difficult material, with determination; let their creative juices flow. Broaden their understanding of mathematics, languages, history, science and fine arts, and give them the ability to apply this understanding to everyday experiences. Let them be willing to ask for help when they need it.

Let them be lifelong learners, who have eyes to see, ears to hear, minds to understand and hearts to discern whatever is true, honorable, just pure, lovely, commendable, excellent and worthy of praise (Philippians 4:8, paraphrased).

In Jesus' Name, we pray.

Amen

Long Distance Grandparenting

Rejoice always, pray without ceasing, give thanks in all circumstances; for this is the will of God in Christ Jesus for you (I Thessalonians 5:16-18).

Abba Father,

We pray you bless our relationship with our long-distance grandchildren. Strengthen the bonds we share with them; bridge the miles between us. Help us discover fun and creative ways to participate in their lives, employing technology when needed. Create opportunities for us to bless them. Show us how to leave a written or recorded spiritual legacy and other such "stones of remembrance" (Joshua 4:1-7) for them to enjoy. Please remind us to pray for them by name every day.

And, when our grandparent hearts ache from missing them, remind us to "rejoice always, pray without ceasing, give thanks in all circumstances (even if we don't understand why they live so far away); for this is the will of God in Christ Jesus" (I Thessalonians 5:15-18).

In Christ's Name, we pray.

Amen.

_____

_____

_____

_____

_____

_____

_____

_____

_____

_____

_____

_____

_____

_____

_____

_____

_____

_____

_____

_____

_____

_____

_____

_____

_____

_____

_____

_____

Marriages of Our Adult Children

What God has joined together, let no one separate (Mark 10:9).

Father God,

We pray our adult children and their spouses honor Your covenant of marriage. Let them be attentive to this covenant, investing the time needed to nurture and maintain a strong relationship with You and each other. "Let (their) marriage bed remain undefiled" (Hebrews 13:4), spiritually, emotionally and physically.

We pray our children and their spouses love one another, sacrificially, as Christ does. Let them treat each other with patience and kindness, without envy or pride. Let them offer each other grace and mercy without a cost. Let them forgive one another, relinquishing their need to have the final word.

We pray they maintain healthy lines of communication, so they can work well as a team. Let them be flexible with their schedules and willing to compromise on things like parenting styles and the family budget. Let them persevere during times of adversity, anchored together in Christ. Let them share a deep and intimate friendship.

In Christ's Name, we pray.

Amen.

Mother's Day

Strength and dignity are her clothing, and she laughs at the time to come (Proverbs 31:25).

Abba Father,

On this Mother's Day weekend, we want to be intentional about thanking you for the mothers of our grandchildren. Some of them are our daughters; others are our daughters-in-law or daughters-in-love. All of them sacrificed, in one way or another, to birth our precious grandchildren.

We pray these busy mothers awaken each morning with the assurance that Your steadfast love never ceases, and Your mercies are fresh (Lamentations 3:22-23). Clothe them in strength, dignity and laughter.

Let them experience the peace of Your Presence, as they juggle children, careers, housework and relationships. Let them "walk in a manner worthy of the Lord, fully pleasing to Him; bearing fruit in every good work and increasing in the knowledge of God" (Colossians 1:10).

Let them fall asleep each night with the assurance that they sleep in the arms of their Savior, as do their children.

In Christ's Name, we pray.

Amen.

_____

_____

_____

_____

_____

_____

_____

_____

_____

_____

_____

_____

_____

_____

_____

_____

_____

_____

_____

_____

_____

_____

_____

_____

_____

_____

_____

New School Year

Fear not, for I am with you; be not dismayed, for I am your God. I will strengthen you; I will help you; I will uphold you with my righteous right hand (Isaiah 41:10).

Abba Father,

We pray for the upcoming school year. Please give the administrators and teachers discerning hearts and minds as they prepare to open the doors on a new year. Let them be wise stewards of the resources at their disposal. Let them make prudent decisions about schedules, curriculum and room assignments. Let them create an environment that is safe, nurturing and conducive for learning.

We also pray for our grandchildren as they prepare to meet this year's teachers, juggle busy schedules, tackle tougher subject matter, renew old friendships and make new ones. We pray they step into the new year, confident that You are with them—strengthening them, helping them and upholding them with your righteous right hand.

In Jesus' Name, we pray.

Amen.

_____

_____

_____

_____

_____

_____

_____

_____

_____

_____

_____

_____

_____

_____

_____

_____

_____

_____

_____

_____

_____

_____

_____

_____

_____

New Year's Day

His mercies never come to an end; they are new every morning (Lamentations 2:22-23).

Father God,

We thank you for new beginnings. We thank you that we don't need a list of New Year's resolutions or a silver ball to drop on Times Square for us to enjoy a fresh start, for You are a redeeming God.

We pray that You chase away any sense of personal failure from our memories of the previous year. We pray that we can forget what lies behind and strain forward to what lies ahead, pressing on toward the goal for the prize of the upward call of God in Christ Jesus" (Philippians 3:13-14, paraphrased).

We pray for opportunities to share our redemption stories with our sons and daughters, our grandsons and granddaughters, so they, too, trust You for their own new beginnings.

In Christ's Name, we pray.

Amen.

_____

_____

_____

_____

_____

_____

_____

_____

_____

_____

_____

_____

_____

_____

_____

_____

_____

_____

_____

_____

_____

_____

_____

_____

_____

_____

_____

Prayer Warriors

The prayer of a righteous person is powerful and effective (James 5:16).

Father God,

Throughout Scripture, we see men and women praying on behalf of others. We see Queen Esther standing in the gap, interceding on behalf of her people. We witness Jesus hanging on the cross, praying for the men who were crucifying Him. We read Paul's words to Timothy, "I urge that supplications, prayers, intercessions and thanksgivings be made for all people" (I Timothy 2:1).

We humbly thank You for calling us to serve as prayer warriors. We thank You for the opportunity to pray on behalf of our families and friends. We thank You for the opportunity to teach our grandchildren how to pray and to share our stories of answered prayer.

We pray You raise up a generation of mighty prayer warriors, namely our grandchildren!

In Christ's Name,

Amen!

_____
_____
_____
_____
_____
_____
_____
_____
_____
_____
_____
_____
_____
_____
_____
_____
_____
_____
_____
_____
_____
_____
_____
_____
_____
_____
_____

Prodigals

"What man of you, having a hundred sheep, if he has lost one of them, does not leave the ninety-nine in the open country, and go after the one that is lost, until he finds it?" (Luke 15:4).

Lord Jesus,

Today, we stand in the gap, interceding for our family members who either don't know you, or like lost sheep, have gone astray. Our hearts ache for their hearts; our minds agonize over their salvation.

You are the Good Shepherd, who promised to search for the lost, even if it's only one. Therefore, we humble ourselves and ask You to find our loved ones and call them back to the fold.

In Your Name, we pray.

Amen.

Protection (1)

He got up and rebuked the wind and the raging waters; the storm subsided, and all was calm (Luke 8:24, NIV).

Lord Jesus,

You are mighty to save!

You know the reality of our grandchildren's storms (physical, emotional or spiritual) even before we mention them by name. Therefore, we call upon Your name, boldly and confidently. We ask You to protect our grandchildren from the enemy's assaults and to rebuke the storms, which Satan's emissaries have placed in their paths.

The victory is yours, for You have overcome the world.

Amen.

_____
_____
_____
_____
_____
_____
_____
_____
_____
_____
_____
_____
_____
_____
_____
_____
_____
_____
_____
_____
_____
_____
_____
_____
_____
_____
_____
_____

Protection (2)

The thief comes only to steal and kill and destroy. I came that they may have life and have it abundantly (John 10:10).

Dearest Lord Jesus,

As we witness another senseless shooting, we recognize the enemy's insatiable desire to steal, kill and destroy innocent people. Our hearts break for the communities of parents, grandparents, teachers and friends who are forced prematurely to say good-bye to their loved ones. Comfort those who grieve. Let Your peace, the peace which passes human understanding, carry them through their dark and tortured days of loss.

These tragedies leave us fearful for our grandchildren's safety. We pray for their protection, as they go to school today, enjoy the playground, visit friends and rest at home. "Guard (them), O LORD, from the hands of the wicked; preserve (them) from violent men, who have planned to trip up (their) feet" (Psalm 140:4).

In Your Name, we pray,

Amen.

Salvation (1)

Arise, O sleeper, and arise from the dead, and Christ will shine on you (Ephesians 5:14).

Dearest Lord Jesus,
We pray you awaken our grandchildren to the Truth of the Gospel message.

Let them understand that You stepped down from the throne of God, took off Your heavenly crown and exchanged Your radiance for human flesh-and-blood. Let them comprehend that You willingly went to Calvary, where You suffered and died for our sin. Let them grasp the significance of the empty tomb from which You were raised on the third day, having conquered sin and death.

Let them receive Your gift of grace and salvation. Let them confess and repent of their sin and invite You into their lives as their Lord and Savior. Let them "walk in newness of life" (Romans 6:4), now and forevermore.

After all, we can't imagine eternity without them.

We pray this prayer in Your Name,

Amen.

Salvation (2)

Whoever confesses that Jesus is the Son of God, God abides in him, and he in God. (I John 4:15)

LORD Jesus,

We pray our grandchildren become confessing Christians.

Let them "believe that You are the Christ, the Son of God" (John 11:27), who came into the world to save sinners. Let them, acknowledging that they "have gone astray and fall short of the glory of God" (Romans 3:26). Let them repent of their sins and return to You. Please wash them in Your blood, clothe them in Your righteousness and anoint them with Your Holy Spirit.

For we long to spend eternity in Your Presence with our grandchildren by our sides.

In Your Name, we pray.

Amen.

_____
_____
_____
_____
_____
_____
_____
_____
_____
_____
_____
_____
_____
_____
_____
_____
_____
_____
_____
_____
_____
_____
_____
_____
_____
_____
_____

Servant Heart

You shall love your neighbor as yourself (Mark 12:30-31).

Father God,

We pray our grandchildren are the body of Christ to a broken world.

Please give them servants' hearts. Let them "do nothing from selfish ambition or conceit, but in humility count others more significant than themselves. Let each look not only to his own interests, but also to the interest of others" (Philippians 2:3-5). Let them be "steadfast, immovable, always abounding in the work of the Lord, knowing that in the Lord (their) labor is not in vain" (I Corinthians 15:58).

Let them spend their days on earth, serving as the hands and feet of Christ

In Jesus' Name, we pray.

Amen.

_____

_____

_____

_____

_____

_____

_____

_____

_____

_____

_____

_____

_____

_____

_____

_____

_____

_____

_____

_____

_____

_____

_____

_____

_____

_____

_____

_____

Spiritual Fitness

And she had a sister called Mary, who sat at the Lord's feet and listened to his teaching… Mary has chosen the good portion, which will not be taken away from her (Luke 10:39, 41-42).

Heavenly Father,

We want to be spiritually fit, not only for ourselves but for our children and grandchildren. We need Your help, though. Give us a taste of Your Presence, stirring in us a desire so strong that we make time with You a priority. Give us the fortitude to withdraw from the world's clamor by unplugging routinely from the distractions vying for our attentions. Refresh us with time spent in Your Presence; replenish us with Your grace.

In Jesus' Name, we pray.

Amen

_____
_____
_____
_____
_____
_____
_____
_____
_____
_____
_____
_____
_____
_____
_____
_____
_____
_____
_____
_____
_____
_____
_____
_____
_____
_____
_____
_____

Teenagers (and Preteens)

Blessed is the man who walks not in the counsel of the wicked, nor stands in the way of sinners, nor sits in the seat of scoffer (Psalm 1:1).;

Heavenly Father,

Today we pray for our grandchildren who are teenagers and preteens. Protect them from any pitfalls, which await them. Pitfalls called identity-crisis, self-worth and peer pressure. Pitfalls persuading them to challenge and rebel against their parents and the values they've been taught.

We pray they choose their friends carefully, for "bad company corrupts good character" (I Corinthians 15:33, *NIV*). We pray they "flee youthful passions and pursue righteousness, faith, love and peace, along with those who call on the Lord from a pure heart" (2 Timothy 2:22).

Please let our grandchildren's identity and self-worth come from You, not their friends.

In Christ's Name, we pray.

Amen.

Thanksgiving

Offer to God a sacrifice of Thanksgiving (Psalm 50:14).

Heavenly Father,

We thank You for the rich spiritual legacy the Pilgrims left us.

(They sailed from England in 1620; their hearts set on religious freedom. After a treacherous 66-day voyage across the Atlantic and brutal first winter in the New World, only half of the original party remained. Spring arrived, along with Squanto and the Wampanoag Indians. Together, they planted seeds and watched the seedlings grow.

The Pilgrims beheld their abundant crops and like the Psalmist asked, "What shall we return to the Lord for all his goodness to us?" (Psalm 116:12, *NIV*). Their answer was a three-day autumn feast thanking You for providing a bountiful harvest.)

We offer You our thanks and praise in the spirit of that inaugural Thanksgiving. We thank You for a year of religious freedom, plentiful harvests, good health, loving relationships and hope for what tomorrow will bring. We praise You for being a merciful Father whose "steadfast love endures forever!" (I Chronicles 16:34).

In Christ's Name, we pray.

Amen.

Walk with God

Noah was a righteous man, blameless in his generation. Noah walked with God (Genesis 6:9).

Father God,

Please plant our grandchildren's feet on the solid ground of sound biblical teaching. "Teach (them) Your way, O Lord, that (they) may walk in Your truth; unite (their) hearts to fear Your name. (Psalm 86:11, *ESV*).

Let them walk as Noah did, blameless and with singleness of heart. Let them forsake all idols. "Direct (their) footsteps according to Your word; let no sin rule over (them)" (Psalm 119:113, *NIV*).

And when they stumble, as we all do, please uphold them in the strength of Your arms.

In Christ's Name, we pray.

Amen.

_____

_____

_____

_____

_____

_____

_____

_____

_____

_____

_____

_____

_____

_____

_____

_____

_____

_____

_____

_____

_____

_____

_____

_____

_____

_____

_____

_____

_____

_____

Wonder

In the beginning, God created the heavens and the earth (Genesis 1:1).

Heavenly Father,

We pray our grandchildren discover the wonder and joy of Your creation. Let them witness the depth, width and breadth of the stars filling the night sky. Let them observe the faithfulness of the sunrise, morning-after-morning. Let them experience the power and intensity of the ocean waves, crashing on the shore. Let them delight in the purity of a cool, mountain brook. Let them savor the sweetness of a watermelon, freshly picked from the garden.

Let them realize that, wherever they look, from the farthest star to the nearest watermelon seed, they are experiencing the magnitude, faithfulness, intensity, purity and sweetness of your perfect and never-ending love.

In Christ's Name, we pray.

Amen.

_____
_____
_____
_____
_____
_____
_____
_____
_____
_____
_____
_____
_____
_____
_____
_____
_____
_____
_____
_____
_____
_____
_____
_____

Author's Note:

I've had a wonderful time assembling these prayers for you. I only wish that we could be sitting in your living room, praying together.

I can't help but wonder how you used the blanks on the right-hand page to make these prayers your own. Did you record the thoughts, which the Holy Spirit brought to your mind? Did you search for other Scripture verses to compliment or replace the ones I included? How did you make these prayers your own?

I wonder also about the miracles you are witnessing in answer to these prayers. Has God awakened your grandchildren to the Truth of the Gospel message? Has He protected them from physical or emotionally harm? Has He carried a wayward child or grandchildren back to the fold?

In closing, I offer one more prayer. It's a prayer for you...

Abba Father,

I thank You for the opportunity to pray with and for these dedicated grandparents. Let them be strong and discerning intercessors, who are committed to pray for their children, grandchildren and grandchildren yet-to-be born. Give these grandparents the courage to pray boldly. And when they don't know how to pray, let "the Spirit Himself intercede for them with groanings too deep for words" (Romans 8:26).

Please use this book to stir their hearts. Encouraging them to write and record their own prayers; prayers that are specific and grounded in the Word of God.

To You, I give the glory.

Amen.

APPENDIX

I've provided two sections of lined space in the appendix for you to further develop your prayer life. The first section is for you to write down verses of Scripture, which "pop-out" when you are reading the Bible, listening to a sermon, reading your devotional, etc. The second section is for you to compose your own prayers with topics of your own choosing. I recommend that you use the verses, you recorded in the first section, to direct you. Don't forget to include these Scriptures in your prayer and to pray the prayers you compose.

SCRIPTURE

_____

_____

_____

_____

_____

_____

_____

_____

_____

_____

_____

_____

_____

_____

_____

_____

_____

_____

_____

_____

_____

_____

_____

_____

_____

_____

_____

_____

_____

_____

_____

_____

_____

_____

_____

_____

_____

_____

_____

_____

_____

_____

_____

_____

_____

_____

_____

_____

_____

PRAYERS

_____

_____

_____

_____

_____

_____

_____

_____

_____

_____

_____

_____

_____

_____

_____

_____

_____

_____

_____

_____

_____

_____

_____

_____

_____

_____

_____
_____
_____
_____
_____
_____
_____
_____
_____
_____
_____
_____
_____
_____
_____
_____
_____
_____
_____
_____
_____
_____
_____

ABOUT THE AUTHOR

Sherry and her husband live in a small, rural town outside of Charleston, South Carolina. They treasure spending time with their three grown sons, three daughters-in-law and five grandchildren.

Sherry serves as the Prayer Director for Christian Grandparenting Network. She has the joy of encouraging grandparents around the world to pray daily for their children and grandchildren. She also serves on staff for the South Carolina GrandCamp, which is a five-day faith adventure designed for grandparents and their grandchildren, ages six to twelve. She is proud to be a charter member of Legacy Coalition.

Sherry wrote the novel entitled *The Christmas Bracelet*. A journey from grief to redemption, it makes readers laugh and cry, sometimes simultaneously. She is in the process of writing *Stepping Up Your Prayer Life: A Grandparent's Expedition in Prayer*.

Sherry invites you to visit her website at www.sherryschumann.com.

Made in the USA
Columbia, SC
20 December 2020

29013974R00062